HOPE JOURNAL

by

Cynthia Owen

Hope Journal
ISBN: 978-0-9971652-3-4
Copyright © 2016 by Cynthia Owen

All rights reserved. No part of this book may be reproduced in any form without permission in writing from the publisher, except in the case of brief quotations embodied in critical articles or reviews.

All Scripture quotations are from the King James Version of the Bible.

Published by:
JC Owen and Associates, Inc.
3558 Round Barn Blvd., Suite 200
Santa Rosa, CA 95403

Printed in the United States of America.

Dear Friend,

As you read through the Hope Journal, you will discover what a powerful word HOPE really is in our daily lives. Hope is like a big pot of soup on your stove's back burner that simmers all day. When you are eager to draw out a hot bowl, it's prepared and ready to eat. Hope is the same way, in that it simmers in your heart. At any time, you can draw on that hope, which God has put in every human heart, to help carry you through life's circumstances. Hope is about trusting God. Trust starts in the heart first, and then at the right time God will manifest what you are trusting him for into your circumstances. It always begins in the heart, followed by the manifestation in the natural realm.

I often think of hope like a wagon: it helps carry us to the finish line! When we are believing God for something specific, hope is one of the keys that will keep us moving forward in faith. Hope causes us to press through difficult obstacles or circumstances that we need to overcome, in order to receive the promise God has for our lives. God is always working behind the scenes in the unseen realm on our behalf.

One specific area that I would like to share with you regarding hope is this: God uses hope as a strategy against the enemy of our souls. What do we do if our dreams or desires are delayed? If we are not careful, we can find ourselves in discouragement or even give up and quit. Discouragement can cause our dreams to be further delayed or possibly not ever come to pass. Delays can cause us to give up because we just become tired of the fight. One reason why Satan works so hard against us with circumstances and delays, is because he knows if he can get us to doubt God and quit, then our dreams will not come to pass. If we remain in hope and faith, and trust God and take him at his word, we stop Satan from stealing our dreams. Satan knows that if he can get us to quit, he has won the battle. DON'T EVER GIVE UP OR QUIT!

If you are fighting against tough circumstances right now in your life, change your FOCUS! Let your hope be strong in your heart today. Focus on God's word and discover faith and hope from God's perspective. Make up your mind that you are going to trust God and stand on his promises. Shut the door to unbelief and doubt. Ask God to increase your faith. The disciples asked God to increase their faith. God didn't give up on them when they were struggling with trying to believe and understand his ability and power. You don't need to worry either, if you feel like you're struggling in your hope and faith. God will work with you, too. The key is getting yourself into hope instead of fear, and allowing your faith to bring the manifestation to you. God is all love and all light. Remember, nothing is impossible with God!

Blessings to you!
Cindy

KEYS TO BUILDING YOUR HOPE

Hope is an unseen power that is within your heart. Always be examining your life to make sure that you are hopeful. Remain in hope; look on the inside of yourself for that strength and power God has put in you.

Let your expectations be focused on Christ meeting your desires, instead of man. Let God bring to pass the desires of your heart.

Don't let delay steal your hope. Delay is a strategy that the enemy uses to try to convince you that God will not answer your prayers.

If you're waiting for God to answer a specific request, don't quit or get discouraged if it takes time for that prayer to be fulfilled.

Set your mind and focus on hope. Be active about keeping your life in hope.

Practice patience. When we have patience in our lives, we are setting ourselves up to receive the desires that are in our heart from God.

Live a life expecting God to be faithful to you.

Always be looking forward and not behind. Hope is always in the future. Paul said to forget those things which are behind you.

God is the one who puts your desires in your heart. Your hope and desires are keys for you to understand what God is trying to bring to pass in your life. Stay in hope and never give up!

HOPE

"For we are saved by hope: but hope that is seen is not hope: for what a man seeth, why doth he yet hope for?"
Romans 8:24

Insights:
_____
_____
_____
_____
_____
_____
_____
_____
_____
_____
_____
_____
_____
_____
_____
_____
_____
_____

Hope

My Declaration: *"Lord, I declare that I'm going to discipline my mind not to look at the circumstances which are seen; I will **put my hope in you.**"*

HOPE

"My soul fainteth for thy salvation: but I hope in thy word."
Psalm 119:81

Insights:
_____
_____
_____
_____
_____
_____
_____
_____
_____
_____
_____
_____
_____
_____
_____
_____
_____
_____

My Declaration: *"Lord, I declare that your word gives me hope for today."*

HOPE

"But sanctify the Lord God in your hearts: and be ready always to give an answer to every man that asketh you a reason of the hope that is in you with meekness and fear ..."
1 Peter 3:15

Insights:

_____
_____
_____
_____
_____
_____
_____
_____
_____
_____
_____
_____
_____
_____
_____
_____
_____
_____

Hope

My Declaration: *"Lord, I declare that I will set my heart toward your word;* **I will consecrate my heart** *to your word. I will have an answer for every man who asks me about the reason I believe in you."*

HOPE

"Hope deferred maketh the heart sick: but when the desire cometh, it is a tree of life."
Proverbs 13:12

Insights:
_____
_____
_____
_____
_____
_____
_____
_____
_____
_____
_____
_____
_____
_____
_____
_____
_____

Hope

My Declaration: *"Lord, I declare that, as I wait patiently for you to bring my desires to pass, **I will not lose hope** and become discouraged because it's taking longer than I thought."*

HOPE

"The eyes of your understanding being enlightened; that ye may know what is the hope of his calling, and what the riches of the glory of his inheritance in the saints ..."
Ephesians 1:18

Insights:

_____

_____

_____

_____

_____

_____

_____

_____

_____

_____

_____

_____

_____

_____

_____

_____

_____

Hope

My Declaration: *"Lord, I declare that I will pursue your kingdom, so that my eyes may be opened. **I want to know** what you are calling me to do, and **I want to see** the direction that you are taking me in my life."*

HOPE

"For we through the Spirit wait for the hope of righteousness by faith."
Galatians 5:5

Insights:
_____
_____
_____
_____
_____
_____
_____
_____
_____
_____
_____
_____
_____
_____
_____
_____
_____
_____

My Declaration: *"Lord, I declare that **I will yield my spirit** to you; it is through your Holy Spirit that I receive everything I need for my daily life."*

HOPE

"According to my earnest expectation and my hope, that in nothing I shall be ashamed, but that with all boldness, as always, so now also Christ shall be magnified in my body, whether it be by life, or by death."
Philippians 1:20

Insights:
_____
_____
_____
_____
_____
_____
_____
_____
_____
_____
_____
_____
_____
_____
_____
_____

My Declaration: *"Lord, I declare that I'm earnestly expecting your glory to be revealed to others **through my life**."*

HOPE

*"When a wicked man dieth, his expectation shall perish:
and the hope of unjust men perisheth."*
Proverbs 11:7

Insights:
_____
_____
_____
_____
_____
_____
_____
_____
_____
_____
_____
_____
_____
_____
_____
_____
_____
_____
_____

My Declaration: *"Lord, I declare that I will go through my life with a continued hope; my expectation will not perish, but will* **be found strong in you."**

HOPE

"And we desire that every one of you do shew the same diligence to the full assurance of hope unto the end ..."
Hebrews 6:11

Insights:

_____
_____
_____
_____
_____
_____
_____
_____
_____
_____
_____
_____
_____
_____
_____
_____
_____
_____

Hope

My Declaration: *"Lord, I declare that my mind will be renewed to the hope of my calling. Let all my diligence and assurance be **found in you** until the end of my life."*

HOPE

*"It is good that a man should both hope
and quietly wait for the salvation of the Lord."
Lamentations 3:26*

Insights:

_____
_____
_____
_____
_____
_____
_____
_____
_____
_____
_____
_____
_____
_____
_____
_____
_____
_____

My Declaration: *"Lord, I declare that, as I wait quietly for you, my hope and faith are strong. I know that, **at the right time**, you will bring to pass the desires of my heart."*

HOPE

"Wherefore gird up the loins of your mind, be sober, and hope to the end for the grace that is to be brought unto you at the revelation of Jesus Christ ..."
1 Peter 1:13

Insights:

_____
_____
_____
_____
_____
_____
_____
_____
_____
_____
_____
_____
_____
_____
_____
_____
_____

Hope

My Declaration: *"Lord, I declare that I will encircle, bind, surround, enclose and hem in **any thought that is against your word**. I will put my hope in you until the end."*

HOPE

*"Uphold me according unto thy word, that I may live:
and let me not be ashamed of my hope."
Psalm 119:116*

Insights:

Hope

My Declaration: "Lord, I declare that my faith and hope are a reflection of your word. **Don't let me waver** back and forth; **don't let my hope be ashamed** because I have chosen to believe your word."

HOPE

"And now abideth faith, hope, charity, these three;
but the greatest of these is charity."
1 Corinthians 13:13

Insights:

My Declaration: *"Lord, I declare that I will offer acts of kindness to others throughout my day;* **I'm going to walk in hope** *during a difficult time by expressing acts of kindness."*

HOPE

*"The hope of the righteous shall be gladness:
but the expectation of the wicked shall perish."
Proverbs 10:28*

Insights:

Hope

My Declaration: *"Lord, I declare that I will offer up praise and gladness throughout the day, because I'm confident that **you will meet all of my expectations**."*

HOPE

*"But if we hope for that we see not,
then do we with patience wait for it."
Romans 8:25*

Insights:
_____
_____
_____
_____
_____
_____
_____
_____
_____
_____
_____
_____
_____
_____
_____
_____

My Declaration: *"Lord, I declare that patience is a key for me to receive the promises you have made me. Just because I don't see the manifestation today doesn't mean that you're not working for me behind the scenes.* **Patience and waiting are both assets in my life.**"

HOPE

*"The wicked is driven away in his wickedness:
but the righteous hath hope in his death."
Proverbs 14:32*

Insights:
_____
_____
_____
_____
_____
_____
_____
_____
_____
_____
_____
_____
_____
_____
_____
_____
_____
_____
_____
_____

Hope

My Declaration: *"Lord, I declare that my righteousness will be found **in you alone**."*

HOPE

*"Blessed is the man that trusteth in the Lord,
and whose hope the Lord is."*
Jeremiah 17:7

Insights:

Hope

My Declaration: *"Lord, I declare that I'm blessed **because I trust you**; my hope will be found in you only. Because I rely on you, I'm blessed!"*

HOPE

*"The Lord is my portion, saith my soul;
therefore will I hope in him."
Lamentations 3:24*

Insights:

Hope

My Declaration: *"Lord, I declare that, because you are my portion, **my soul is full and at peace**. I have no fear, because I trust you with my life; my hope is in you."*

HOPE

"Thou art wearied in the greatness of thy way; yet saidst thou not, There is no hope: thou hast found the life of thine hand; therefore thou wast not grieved."
Isaiah 57:10

Insights:
_____
_____
_____
_____
_____
_____
_____
_____
_____
_____
_____
_____
_____
_____
_____
_____
_____
_____

My Declaration: *"Lord, I declare that, when I find myself in a weary and troublesome situation, **I will not worry**, because my hope is in you. You will give me wisdom and guidance through **any difficult situation.**"*

HOPE

"And hope maketh not ashamed; because the love of God is shed abroad in our hearts by the Holy Ghost which is given unto us."
Romans 5:5

Insights:
_____
_____
_____
_____
_____
_____
_____
_____
_____
_____
_____
_____
_____
_____
_____
_____
_____
_____
_____

My Declaration: "*Lord, I declare that I will be confident and not ashamed, **because I'm loved by you**. Your Spirit fully permeates my heart; you have given me your Holy Spirit to **guide me through life**.*"

HOPE

*"Seest thou a man that is hasty in his words?
There is more hope of a fool than of him."*
Proverbs 29:20

Insights:

Hope

My Declaration: *"Lord, I declare that I will be slow to speak, and **I will use words of wisdom**. I won't make any quick, rash decisions; I will get all the details and facts before I decide on anything."*

HOPE

*"I wait for the Lord, my soul doth wait,
and in his word do I hope."*
Psalm 130:5

Insights:

My Declaration: *"Lord, I declare that I don't mind waiting for you;* ***I know you are working on my behalf.****"*

HOPE

"Rejoicing in hope; patient in tribulation; continuing instant in prayer ..."
Romans 12:12

Insights:

My Declaration: *"Lord, I declare that you will find me rejoicing in my hope.* **I will remain in patience** *when I'm found in a trial, and* **I will continue** *to lift up my voice to you in prayer."*

HOPE

"If ye continue in the faith grounded and settled, and be not moved away from the hope of the gospel, which ye have heard ..."
Colossians 1:23

Insights:
_____
_____
_____
_____
_____
_____
_____
_____
_____
_____
_____
_____
_____
_____
_____
_____
_____
_____
_____
_____
_____

My Declaration: *"Lord, I declare that I am grounded and settled in the gospel. Never let me be found wavering or moving away from **the hope of the gospel**."*

HOPE

"But I would not have you to be ignorant, brethren, concerning them which are asleep, that ye sorrow not, even as others which have no hope."
1 Thessalonians 4:13

Insights:

_____
_____
_____
_____
_____
_____
_____
_____
_____
_____
_____
_____
_____
_____
_____
_____
_____

My Declaration: *"Lord, I declare that **I will not sorrow** like those who have no hope."*

HOPE

*"The Lord taketh pleasure in them that fear him,
in those that hope in his mercy."
Psalm 147:11*

Insights:

Hope

My Declaration: *"Lord, I declare that I'm excited that you take pleasure in me **because I hope in your mercy**. I have my heart **turned in reverence** toward you."*

HOPE

"Looking for that blessed hope, and the glorious appearing of the great God and our Saviour Jesus Christ ..."
Titus 2:13

Insights:

My Declaration: *"Lord, I declare that **I will be found working** in your kingdom when you return. I will be out in the fields sharing your gospel, and sharing your hope."*

HOPE

*"Be not a terror unto me:
thou art my hope in the day of evil."
Jeremiah 17:17*

Insights:
_____
_____
_____
_____
_____
_____
_____
_____
_____
_____
_____
_____
_____
_____
_____
_____
_____

My Declaration: *"Lord, I declare that, in the day of evil, **I will not be afraid**. I will not let terror allow a spirit of fear to come into my life."*

HOPE

"Therefore did my heart rejoice, and my tongue was glad; moreover also my flesh shall rest in hope ..."
Acts 2:26

Insights:

My Declaration: "*Lord, I declare that my heart is in joy, and the confession of my mouth is good;* **I have an amazing hope in you.**"

HOPE

"That at that time ye were without Christ, being aliens from the commonwealth of Israel, and strangers from the covenants of promise, having no hope, and without God in the world ..."
Ephesians 2:12

Insights:

Hope

My Declaration: *"Lord, I declare that I'm no longer alienated from your presence; I gave my life to you,* **and now I'm in your kingdom.***"*

HOPE

"The Lord also shall roar out of Zion, and utter his voice from Jerusalem; and the heavens and the earth shall shake: but the Lord will be the hope of his people, and the strength of the children of Israel."
Joel 3:16

Insights:

Hope

My Declaration: *"Lord, I declare that, even if the earth is removed and falls into the sea, **I will be confident in you**. I will be still, and know that **you are God**."*

HOPE

"For whatsoever things were written aforetime were written for our learning, that we through patience and comfort of the scriptures might have hope."
Romans 15:4

Insights:

_____
_____
_____
_____
_____
_____
_____
_____
_____
_____
_____
_____
_____
_____
_____
_____

My Declaration: *"Lord, I declare that your word gives me comfort.* **I have put my hope in you**; *your scriptures will lead and guide me into all truth."*

HOPE

"That being justified by his grace, we should be made heirs according to the hope of eternal life."
Titus 3:7

Insights:

Hope

My Declaration: *"Lord, I declare that I will press forward to reach for the inheritance that you have given to me. **I have hope in your ability** to bring to pass everything that you want me to accomplish."*

HOPE

"Therefore I will look unto the Lord; I will wait for the God of my salvation: my God will hear me."
Micah 7:7

Insights:

_____

_____

_____

_____

_____

_____

_____

_____

_____

_____

_____

_____

_____

_____

_____

_____

_____

_____

_____

_____

My Declaration: *"Lord, **I declare that I trust you.**"*

HOPE

"Who against hope believed in hope, that he might become the father of many nations; according to that which was spoken, So shall thy seed be."
Romans 4:18

Insights:

Hope

My Declaration: *"Lord, I declare that, because I choose to believe, **I will see the promises of the Lord.**"*